What We Do in Spring

by JoAnn Early Macken

LOOK!
BOOKS™

Red Chair Press   Egremont, Massachusetts

Look! Books are produced and published by Red Chair Press:

Red Chair Press LLC   PO Box 333   South Egremont, MA 01258-0333

www.redchairpress.com

FREE activity page from www.redchairpress.com/free-activities

Publisher's Cataloging-In-Publication Data

Names: Macken, JoAnn Early, 1953-

Title: What we do in spring / by JoAnn Early Macken.

Description: Egremont, Massachusetts : Red Chair Press, [2018] | Series: Look! books : Seasons can be fun | Interest age level: 004-007. | Includes Now You Know fact-boxes, a glossary, and resources for additional reading. | Includes index. | Summary: "Making personal connections to seasonal activity is a powerful way for young readers to learn how each season differs from the others... Do you like planting a garden? Maybe you like flying a kite. Let's discover all the fun things to do in Spring."--Provided by publisher.

Identifiers: ISBN 978-1-63440-306-1 (library hardcover) | ISBN 978-1-63440-358-0 (paperback) | ISBN 978-1-63440-310-8 (ebook)

Subjects: LCSH: Spring--Juvenile literature. | Amusements--Juvenile literature. | CYAC: Spring. | Amusements.

Classification: LCC QB637.4 .M334 2018 (print) | LCC QB637.4 (ebook) | DDC 508.2 [E]--dc23

LCCN 2017947526

Illustration on p. 16 by Joe LeMonnier

Photo credits: Cover, p. 1, 3, 7, 9, 15, 17, 18, 19, 21, 22, 23, 24: iStock; p. 4, 5, 8, 9, 10, 11, 12, 13, 14, 15, 24: Shutterstock

Printed in the United States of America

0718 1P CGF18

Table of Contents

A Wet Season

Spring begins in March. Spring can be a wet season. Snow melts, and **icicles** drip. We watch rain fall from dark clouds. Can you name the months of Spring?

MARCH						
M	T	W	T	F	S	
	1	2	3	4	5	
7	8	9	10	11	12	
14	15	16	17	18	19	
21	22	23	24	25	26	
28	29	30				

APRIL						
M	T	W	T	F	S	S
				1	2	3	4
5	6	7	8	9	10	11
12	13	14	15	16	17	18
19	20	21	22	23	24	25
26	27	28	29	30	31	

MAY						
T	W	T	F	S	S	
					1	
3	4	5	6	7	8	
10	11	12	13	14	15	
17	18	19	20	21	22	
24	25	26	27	28	29	

Outside in Spring

We wear raincoats and boots to play outside. Puddles form on the paths. We run and jump and *SPLASH!*

We take a **nature** walk in the park. We look for toads in the woods. We look for frogs at the pond. We find turtles on a sunny rock.

Good to Know

Frogs spend time in water. They have smooth, wet skin. A toad's skin is bumpy and dry.

We watch a robin build a nest. She carries grass and twigs into a tree. She lays eggs in the nest. She sits on the eggs to keep them warm.

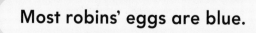
Most robins' eggs are blue.

Green and Growing

Plants grow in spring. We see tulips and lilacs. Apple and cherry trees bloom. Tiny green buds on trees turn into new leaves.

We buy seeds for our garden. We plant one row of peas. We plant one row of beets. We plant one row of carrots. How many rows do we plant?

Seedlings are young
plants started from seeds.

Wiggly Worms

In school, we learn about worms. They wiggle and tickle! Worms are good for the earth. They break down dead plants and **animals**. Worms make space for roots to grow.

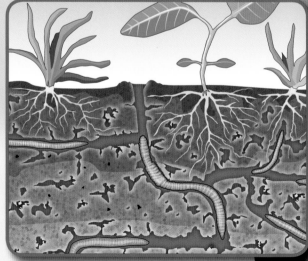

Windy Playground

At recess, we jump rope.
We play hopscotch.
The wind blows our hair.
The wind bends the
treetops. It lifts kites
up high.

Good to Know

Kites were invented in China more than 2,000 years ago! April is National Kite Flying Month.

Spring Can be Fun

We decorate our classroom for Spring. We make flowers, birds and kites to hang on the walls.

Words to Keep

animal: a living being that can move and breathe

icicle: hanging ice that forms when dripping water freezes

nature: plants, animals, land, and the rest of the world other than what people have made

Learn More at the Library

Books (Check out these books to learn more.)

Latta, Sara L. *Why Is It Spring?* Enslow Publishing, 2012.

Moon, Walter K. *Spring Is Fun! (Bumba Books)* Lerner Publications, 2017.

Murray, Julie. *Spring.* Abdo Kids, 2016.

Nelson, Robin. *Seasons (Discovering Nature's Cycles)* Lerner Publications, 2011.

Web Sites (Ask an adult to show you these web sites.)

Easy Science for Kids
http://easyscienceforkids.com/all-about-seasons/

University of Illinois: Tree House Weather Kids
https://extension.illinois.edu/treehouse/seasons.cfm?Slide=1

Index

About the Author

JoAnn Early Macken has written more than 130 books for young children. She enjoys taking walks in the Spring showers at home in Wisconsin.